SPOTLIGHT ON
CIVIC COURAGE
HEROES OF CONSCIENCE™

NELSON MANDELA

SOUTH AFRICAN PRESIDENT AND ANTI-APARTHEID ACTIVIST

Susan Meyer

Rosen
YA™

New York

Published in 2018 by The Rosen Publishing Group, Inc.
29 East 21st Street, New York, NY 10010

Library of Congress Cataloging-in-Publication Data

Names: Meyer, Susan, 1986– author.
Title: Nelson Mandela : South African president and anti-apartheid activist / Susan Meyer.
Description: New York : Rosen YA, 2018. | Series: Spotlight on civic courage : heroes of conscience | Audience: Grades 5–10. | Includes bibliographical references and index.
Identifiers: LCCN 2017013018| ISBN 9781538380918 (library bound) | ISBN 9781538380888 (pbk.) | ISBN 9781538380895 (6 pack)
Subjects: LCSH: Mandela, Nelson, 1918–2013—Juvenile literature. | Presidents—South Africa—Biography—Juvenile literature. | Anti-apartheid activists—South Africa—Biography—Juvenile literature. | Political prisoners—South Africa—Biography—Juvenile literature. | South Africa—Politics and government—1948–1994—Juvenile literature. | South Africa—Politics and government—1994-—Juvenile literature.
Classification: LCC DT1974 .M49 2018 | DDC 968.06092—dc23
LC record available at https://lccn.loc.gov/2017013018

Manufactured in the United States of America

On the cover: This photo of Mandela was taken in 1994, at a pre-election rally during the weeks leading up to South Africa's first true democratic election. The background image shows a march in 1976 in Soweto, during the period in which apartheid was still the law of the land.

CONTENTS

A Champion of Equality

Nelson Mandela was a man who fought tirelessly for equality in his homeland of South Africa. For much of Mandela's life, South Africa was under a system of segregation called apartheid. Under apartheid, people were judged by the color of their skin. Most of the population of the country was black, but white people controlled the government. The government restricted the rights of black people through a number of laws and policies.

Mandela spent most of his life trying to end apartheid. He was a believer in nonviolent resistance, where possible, as a way to achieve change. He spent twenty-seven years of his life in prison for his beliefs. But eventually his fight would be rewarded. Apartheid was outlawed in 1994. Mandela went on to become the first black president of South Africa and even won the Nobel Peace Prize for his role in ending apartheid.

Nelson Mandela was imprisoned for almost three decades because of his role in the fight against an unjust system. This photo was taken in 1990, a few months after his release.

A COLONIAL PAST

Before looking at the life of Mandela, it is important to understand a little about the history of the country where he was born—a country he would spend his life fighting for. People have inhabited the land that is now South Africa for 2.5 million years. The area eventually became home to several ethnic groups, including the San, Xhosa, and Zulu peoples.

The land first caught the eye of European explorers in the fifteenth century. Dutch ships began stopping there on their way to India, and Dutch settlers followed in the seventeenth century. Later, the British set up colonies. The British eventually fought two wars against descendants of Dutch settlers, called the Boers.

Over the centuries, both the British and the Boers fought with the native peoples, who had lived on the land for thousands of years. Imagine what it would be like for someone to come to the land your family had lived on for generations and suddenly say it was theirs.

This painting shows the Battle of Rorke's Drift, which took place in January 1879. It was part of the Anglo-Zulu War, which ended with the defeat of the Zulu Kingdom by the forces of the British Empire.

This map shows South Africa as it existed in 1912. At that point in time, most of this land was under British control.

By the nineteenth century, South Africa was divided into various colonies, kingdoms, and republics. The British eventually conquered nearly all of the area and united it into a single country in 1910, called the Union of South Africa.

This new country was full of harsh laws based on segregation and racism. Only a small percentage of land was set aside for black people, even though they made up the majority of the people in the country. Colonists accounted for 20 percent of the population, but they took 90 percent of the land available.

Nelson Mandela was born eight years after the creation of the Union of South Africa. He was born into a country where his land could be taken, where he wasn't allowed to go to the same schools as white people, and where he was wasn't allowed to vote in elections. As he grew up, Mandela would spend his life working to change all of this.

The Boy from Transkei

Mandela was born on July 18, 1918, in the village of Mvezo in the Transkei region of South Africa. His birth name was Rolihlahla. In the Xhosa language, *Rolihlahla* means "trouble-maker." It wasn't until he went to school at the age of seven that his teacher gave him the name Nelson.

Mandela was born into the Madiba clan. His father, Nkosi Mphakanyiswa Gadla Mandela, was a chief of the Tembu people. His mother, Nonqaphi Nosekeni, was his father's third wife. Nelson had nine brothers and sisters.

When Nelson was twelve years old, his father died. The young boy was taken under the wing of a high leader of the Tembu named Jongintaba Dalindyebo. He made sure Nelson received the best schooling, and he wanted to prepare Nelson for a life of leadership. Through him, Nelson learned stories of his ancestors' past wars of resistance. The young Nelson looked forward to one day having his own impact.

This is the hut in Mvezo where Nelson Mandela was born. Shortly after his birth, his father lost his position of power in the town and the family moved to nearby Qunu.

THE YOUNG STUDENT

Mandela attended school in the nearby town of Qunu, where he lived with his mother and siblings after his father's death. He then moved to nearby Headtown to attend high school. After high school, he attended the University College of Fort Hare. This was a top college for black South Africans. Mandela made strong friendships there and began to take part in activism.

Many of the students at Fort Hare later played a role in the fight to end apartheid. One of them was Oliver Tambo. He and Mandela met as students and became lifelong friends.

During his first year at Fort Hare, Mandela became involved in a student strike along with his friend Tambo because they were unhappy with the food served in the cafeteria. This was a comparatively minor issue, but it demonstrates Mandela's early willingness to stand up for what he believed in. The school wasn't happy about the stand the students took against it. The school expelled both Mandela and Tambo.

Oliver Tambo, seen here in 1960, would become one of Nelson Mandela's lifelong friends and a fellow resistance fighter in the movement against apartheid.

As a young man, Mandela developed a love for boxing and long-distance running. He would later write, "I did not enjoy the violence of boxing so much as the science of it."

Mandela had no choice but to go home. When he got there, he discovered that Jongintaba Dalindyebo was planning an arranged marriage for him. Mandela decided he wasn't ready to get married, so he fled to the big city of Johannesburg. He worked as a guard at a diamond mine and later as a clerk in a law office. While working, Mandela knew that he still wanted to complete the degree he had started at Fort Hare. He signed up for a correspondence course at the University of South Africa. This meant that he could complete his degree by mailing in his assignments.

Mandela completed his college courses and received a bachelor's degree in 1943. He was still working at the law firm, and he decided he wanted to continue his education by attending law school. He started studying at the University of the Witwatersrand, but he would not complete the degree.

Joining the Party

In Johannesburg, Mandela was discovering a world very different from what he had known in the villages of his childhood. He encountered new people and new ideas. One of these people was Walter Sisulu, who worked with Mandela at the law firm.

In 1944, Mandela, along with his friends Sisulu and Tambo, joined the African National Congress, also known as the ANC. The ANC is a political party that became a mass movement working to end apartheid. It worked to defy apartheid by organizing boycotts, protests, and strikes. The South African government tried to prevent people from joining the ANC and even banned it. Mandela first helped the group by working with the ANC Youth League. He served as the secretary of the Youth League in 1948 and would later serve as its president.

During this time, Mandela also married Sisulu's cousin Evelyn Mase. They would have two sons and two daughters, although one daughter died in infancy.

Walter Sisulu was an important anti-apartheid activist. He served as secretary general and later deputy president of the ANC. He was a political prisoner on Robben Island for twenty-six years.

A Policy of Injustice

To understand the anti-apartheid movement, it is important to first understand a little of the background around the policy. "Apartheid" means "apartness," which makes it a fitting name for a policy of segregation. Apartheid was officially begun by the South African National Party in 1948. Under apartheid, the government classified people by race. Black South Africans were denied rights because they were black. They were told where they could live and sometimes were forcibly removed from their land so that it could be given to white farmers.

The apartheid government tried to end the defiance from the ANC. In 1952, Mandela served the ANC cause by traveling

around the country looking for volunteers willing to break the unjust laws of apartheid. One of their first acts of defiance was to break curfew restrictions. The apartheid government required all black people to return to their homes by a certain time. Mandela and other activists would be arrested many times for their defiance.

This 1950 photo shows children looking through a barbed wire fence marking a township border in Soweto. Apartheid created segregation in South Africa through both physical and legal barriers.

Fighting Back Without Violence

The ANC movement aimed to end apartheid without violence. They hoped to bring understanding and change without using the same methods that were used against them.

There are examples throughout history of people managing to change unjust circumstances without wars and bloodshed. While Mandela was fighting racism in South Africa, Martin Luther King Jr. was doing the same—using nonviolent resistance strategies such as boycotts and protests—in the United States.

Mandela and the ANC may also have been inspired by the movement led by Mahatma Gandhi to free India from British rule. In fact, Gandhi's son Manilal spent time in South Africa trying to encourage the movement to avoid using violence.

In this 1956 photo, Martin Luther King Jr. (*center*) calls for calmness after an attack on his home. This was in the midst of the Montgomery bus boycott, an act of nonviolent resistance during the American civil rights movement.

Mandela believed in nonviolence, but he also felt it had its limits. He is quoted as saying, "Nonviolent passive resistance is effective as long as your opposition adheres to the same rules as you do." The apartheid government was not afraid to use violence to end defiance.

THE TREASON TRIAL

In 1955, the police arrested 156 anti-apartheid activists. Mandela was among them. The group was rounded up and taken to Johannesburg, where they were kept in Fort Prison.

The government wanted to end the resistance once and for all. It picked special judges to oversee the trial. Mandela and the others were charged with attempting to overthrow the government. The Freedom Charter was used as evidence of the plan.

The charges amounted to treason, and the resulting court hearings would become known as the Treason Trial. The trial would drag on for several years. Mandela used his legal training

to play a role in the group's defense during the trial. Finally in 1961, the judges all agreed that Mandela and the other activists were innocent of treason. Mandela was free.

During the trial, Mandela and his wife, Evelyn, divorced. In 1958, he married his second wife, a social worker named Winnie Madikizela.

Here Mandela (*third from left*) and other leaders from the ANC are seen walking into Drill Hall in Johannesburg, where their treason trial was held.

THE SHARPEVILLE MASSACRE

While the Treason Trial went on, events in South Africa were coming to a head. In 1960, a group of five thousand black protesters in the township of Sharpeville gathered to speak out against pass laws. Pass laws required black South Africans to carry identification documents with them at all times. This helped the government restrict where they traveled within the country.

The peaceful protest turned deadly when the group approached a police station and the police opened fire on the crowd, killing sixty-nine people. This event became known as the Sharpeville Massacre.

The massacre was very difficult for Mandela to learn about. He and some of the other leaders of the movement began to doubt that nonviolent resistance could work in South Africa, when their peaceful efforts were met with such violence in return. Feeling he had no choice, Mandela helped set up a military branch of the ANC called Umkhonto we Sizwe, which means "Spear of the Nation."

Peaceful protesters were forced to flee for their lives when South African police opened fire on the crowd during the Sharpeville Massacre.

TAKEN PRISONER

In January of 1962, Mandela left South Africa to go to England. He wanted to build support for the anti-apartheid movement abroad. On his return to South Africa, he was arrested because he had left the country without permission from the government. He was sentenced to five years in jail. He would begin serving his sentence in 1963 in a prison in Pretoria.

While he was in jail, several of the other ANC leaders were arrested in a raid. Mandela was sent to join them on trial for sabotage and attempting to overthrow the government. The group faced the death penalty, but Mandela was not afraid. In a 1964 speech, he said, "I have cherished the ideal of a democratic and free society in which all persons live together in harmony and with equal opportunities. It is an ideal which I hope to live for and to achieve. But if needs be, it is an ideal for which I am prepared to die."

Mandela left South Africa illegally because he wanted to gain support for the anti-apartheid movement abroad. Here he is in London, England, in the early 1960s.

On June 11, 1964, Mandela and seven others, including Walter Sisulu, were sentenced to life in prison. They were sent to Robben Island, off the coast of Cape Town, to serve out their sentences. Robben Island housed mostly political prisoners.

Robben Island sits in Table Bay, off the coast of Cape Town. The island is only 2 square miles (5 square kilometers) in area. Today, it is a UNESCO World Heritage Site.

Political prisoners are those who are jailed because of their political beliefs and actions. These people are often activists that a government is attempting to silence. From 1964 until 1982, Mandela was kept in a tiny cell on Robben Island. In

1982, he was moved to Pollsmoor Prison in Cape Town, where he was kept until his release on February 11, 1990. He refused earlier offers to be released because he didn't want to be released while the government was still under apartheid rule.

Mandela gave up his freedom, but he helped raise awareness for the cause. Countries around the world took notice of the way Mandela was treated. They called for his release and put pressure on the South African government to end apartheid.

A NEW SOUTH AFRICA

Mandela's release in 1990 was a sign that things were changing in South Africa. The ANC, which had long been banned by the government, was now allowed. Mandela immediately began assisting the talks to help finally end apartheid once and for all. In 1991, he was elected president of the ANC. He took over the role from his old friend Oliver Tambo, who had returned to South Africa after living in exile and who was in poor health.

In 1993, Mandela and F. W. de Klerk jointly won the Nobel Peace Prize for their work in negotiating an end to nearly a century of organized racism. De Klerk was the last president of South Africa under apartheid.

In 1994, apartheid finally ended in South Africa, in no small part due to Mandela's efforts. On April 27, 1994, Mandela was able to vote for the first time in his life as South Africa held its first democratic elections.

Nelson Mandela and his wife, Winnie, celebrate his release from Victor Verster Prison (to which he had been moved in late 1988) in this famous photograph from 1990.

South Africa's First Black President

The people of the new democratic South Africa voted for Mandela to be their president. He was inaugurated on May 10, 1994. The ceremony was attended by world leaders and over one hundred thousand people. It was shown live on television all over the world. In his speech to the people, Mandela said that he would help to heal the country and continue to fight against discrimination.

Mandela moved into the presidential offices in Cape Town. He didn't feel he needed his full salary as president and donated a third of it to a foundation he had established in 1995 called Nelson Mandela's Children's Fund.

A primary goal of Mandela's presidency was reuniting the country after so many years of division. He wanted to

Mandela visited the United States in 1994, a few months after the end of apartheid. Here he is speaking at the White House while US president Bill Clinton looks on.

assure white South Africans that they, too, had an equal place in the new South Africa, which he called "the Rainbow Nation." He set in motion the creation of a new flag to symbolize the many people who make up South Africa.

TRUTH.

THE ROAD TO

RECONCILIATION

Mandela (*left*) stands with Desmond Tutu, who headed the Truth and Reconciliation Commission. In October 1998, Tutu gave Mandela the TRC's final report.

Having achieved what he had worked so hard for, Mandela did not want to punish those responsible for the discrimination under apartheid. Instead, he wanted to reach a place of forgiveness and reconciliation. Under Mandela's government, a new constitution of South Africa was created in 1996.

As part of his goal of bringing together white and black South Africans, Mandela formed a new group called the Truth and Reconciliation Commission. Its job was to investigate crimes that had been committed under apartheid. The TRC gave amnesty to many that had committed crimes if they testified.

Mandela's calls for unity helped calm the fears of white South Africans, but some black South Africans felt that he was being too forgiving. One person who felt this way was Mandela's own wife, Winnie. Their differences would eventually lead them to divorce. On his eightieth birthday in 1998, Mandela married his third wife, Graça Machel.

A FORCE FOR GOOD

Mandela served as president for five years. In 1997, he gave up his role as ANC president, and in 1999, he chose not to run for a second term as president of South Africa. He planned to retire to Johannesburg and Qunu.

In 1994, he had written an autobiography called *Long Walk to Freedom*. The book talked about his time in prison. It became an international best seller. During his retirement, Mandela worked on a sequel to the book about his time as president, but he never finished it.

Although he was retired, Mandela never really stopped working.

He devoted himself to helping people. He particularly focused on the issues of combatting HIV/AIDS and providing scholarships for African students. He started a campaign to raise global awareness about AIDS, which he called 46664. This was his prisoner number during all his years of imprisonment.

Mandela continued to champion for causes he believed in after his presidency ended. Here he speaks at the International AIDS conference in 2002 about the plight of AIDS orphans.

MANDELA'S LEGACY

Nelson Mandela died at his home in Johannesburg on December 5, 2013. His death was mourned all over the world.

He was a true example of the courage of one's convictions. He didn't give up on what he believed in, even though it meant sacrificing decades of his personal freedom. He fought tirelessly to end a system of organized racism. Mandela transformed the country he loved from one ruled by segregation and discrimination to one in which people have equal rights regardless of the color of their skin.

Nelson Mandela was able to accomplish much of what he did through nonviolent defiance. He recognized injustice and never stopped rallying against it. Consider Mandela's legacy when you encounter injustice in the world around you. Know that you can always speak out about the wrongs you see in the world and try to right them, just as Mandela spent his life doing.

Nelson Mandela always believed that an unjust system could be changed. Here he is photographed just a few days before the official end of apartheid in 1994.

GLOSSARY

activism Taking action to bring about political or social change.

amnesty Granting pardons to people who are accused of political crimes.

apartheid A South African system of government defined by segregation and racist policies that operated from 1910 to 1994.

arranged marriage When two people who don't know each other agree to marry, usually set up by their families.

boycott To refuse to use a good or service for political reasons.

clan A group of families with shared ancestors.

colony An area of land that is taken under control by another country.

convictions Deeply held beliefs.

curfew A time after which people are not allowed to be outside of their homes.

defy To openly disobey authority.

ethnic group A group of people who have a shared culture, language, history, and traditions.

exile To be forced to leave one's country.

expel To be forced to leave one's school.

massacre The mass murder of a large group of people.

reconciliation Returning to friendly relations after a conflict.

resign To give up an office or post.

segregation Rules or policies that keep people apart and give them access to different goods and services based on race or background.

strike Refusal to work as a way to impact change.

township In South Africa under apartheid, this was a neighborhood where black people were told to live.

treason The betrayal of one's country.

FOR MORE INFORMATION

American Civil Liberties Union
125 Broad Street, 18th Floor
New York, NY 10004
(212) 549-2500
Website: https://www.aclu.org
Facebook: @aclu.nationwide
Twitter: @ACLU
The ACLU is a nonpartisan, nonprofit organization whose mission is to defend the rights and liberties of everyone. Like Nelson Mandela, the ACLU fights for equal rights and justice for all people regardless of race and background.

Canadian Human Rights Commission
344 Slater Street, 8th Floor
Ottawa, ON K1A 1E1
Canada
(888) 214-1090
Website: http://www.chrc-ccdp.gc.ca
Facebook: @CanadianHumanRightsCommission
Twitter: @CdnHumanRights
Established in 1977 by the Canadian government, this group supports the Canadian Human Rights Act by protecting the human rights of all Canadian citizens and investigating instances of discrimination.

Human Rights First
75 Broad Street, 31st Floor
New York, NY 10004
(212) 845-5200
Website: http://www.humanrightsfirst.org
Facebook: @humanrightsfirst
Twitter: @humanrights1st
This nonprofit human rights organization is committed to defending human rights around the world, including fighting hate crimes, war crimes, and crimes against humanity.

Nelson Mandela Foundation

Private Bag X70000

Houghton 2041

South Africa

Website: https://www.nelsonmandela.org

Facebook: @NelsonMandelaCentreOfMemory

Twitter: @NelsonMandela

This nonprofit organization is dedicated to preserving the memory, dialogue, and legacy of Nelson Mandela. The foundation also works to promote Mandela's vision of equality for all.

United Nations

405 East 42nd Street

New York, NY 10017

(212) 963-9999

Website: http://www.un.org/en

Facebook: @UnitedNations

Twitter: @UN

The United Nations is an international organization that was founded in 1945 to help governments in its member nations work together to solve world problems. Mandela made a landmark speech to the United Nations in 1994 about the end of apartheid.

WEBSITES

Because of the changing nature of Internet links, Rosen Publishing has developed an online list of websites related to the subject of this book. This site is updated regularly. Please use this link to access the list:

http://www.rosenlinks.com/CIVC/Mandela

FOR FURTHER READING

Baptiste, Tracey. *Nelson Mandela: Nobel Peace Prize-Winning Champion for Hope and Harmony* (Britannica Beginner Bios). New York, NY: Britannica Educational Publishing, 2016.

Belviso, Meg, and Pamela D. Pollack. *Who Was Nelson Mandela?* New York, NY: Grosset & Dunlap, 2014.

Capozzi, Suzy. *Nelson Mandela: From Prisoner to President.* New York, NY: Penguin Random House, 2016.

Chalk, Frank. *South Africa* (Genocide and Persecution). Farmington Hills, MI: Greenhaven Press, 2014.

Gormley, Beatrice. *Nelson Mandela: South Africa Revolutionary.* New York, NY: Aladdin, 2016.

Keller, Bill. *Tree Shaker: The Story of Nelson Mandela.* New York, NY: Macmillan, 2013.

Malaspina, Ann. *Nelson Mandela: Fighting to Dismantle Apartheid* (Rebels with a Cause). New York, NY: Enslow Publishing, 2017.

Mandela, Nelson. *Long Walk to Freedom: The Autobiography of Nelson Mandela.* Boston, MA: Back Bay Books, 1995.

Nepstad, Sharon. *Nonviolent Struggle: Theories, Strategies, and Dynamics.* New York, NY: Oxford University Press, 2015.

Perritano, John. *South Africa* (Major Nations in a Global World: Tradition, Culture, and Daily Life). Broomall, PA: Mason Crest, 2016.

Rajczak, Kristen. *Nelson Mandela* (Heroes of Black History). New York, NY: Gareth Stevens Publishing, 2016.

Woll, Kris. *Nelson Mandela: South African President and Civil Rights Activist.* Mankato, MN: Core Library, 2015.

BIBLIOGRAPHY

Boehmer, Elleke. *Nelson Mandela: A Very Short Introduction.* New York, NY: Oxford University Press, 2008.

Clark, Nancy L., and William H. Worger. *South Africa: The Rise and Fall of Apartheid.* New York, NY: Routledge, 2004.

Gandhi, M. K. *Non-Violent Resistance.* Mineola, NY: Dover Publications, 2001.

Kathrada, Ahmed, and Tim Couzens. *A Simple Freedom: The Strong Mind of Robben Island Prisoner No. 468/64.* Lexington, KY: University of Kentucky Press, 2016.

Mandela, Nelson. *Conversations with Myself.* New York, NY: Farrar, Straus, and Giroux, 2010.

Mandela, Nelson. *The Struggle Is My Life.* New York, NY: Pathfinder, 1986.

Meredith, Martin. *Diamonds, Gold, and War: The British, the Boers, and the Making of South Africa.* New York, NY: Perseus Book Group, 2008.

Nelson Mandela Foundation. "Life and Times of Nelson Mandela." Retrieved February 20, 2017. https://www.nelsonmandela.org/landing/life-and-times.

Sampson, Anthony. *Mandela: The Authorized Biography.* New York, NY: Random House, 2000.

INDEX

About the Author

Susan Meyer is an author of more than twenty young adult titles. In 2007, she spent six months living in South Africa learning about conflict resolution, the TRC, and the fascinating history of this amazingly resilient country. While there, she visited Robben Island and Nelson Mandela's prison cell. She found the experience extremely moving as a reminder of what brave men have struggled through to impact change. Meyer currently lives in Austin, Texas, with her husband, Sam, and cat, Dinah.

Photo Credits

Cover (portrait) Per-Anders Pettersson/Hulton Archive/Getty Images; cover (background) AFP/Getty Images; p. 5 Michel Clement/AFP/Getty Images; pp. 6–7, 17, 26–27 Universal History Archive/Universal Images Group/Getty Images; pp. 8–9 Antiqua Print Gallery/Alamy Stock Photo; pp. 10–11 Foto24/Gallo Images/Getty Images; p. 13 © Topham/The Image Works; p. 14 Keystone/Hulton Archive/Getty Images; pp. 18–19 Margaret Bourke-White/The LIFE Picture Collection/Getty Images; p. 21 Bettmann/Getty Images; pp. 22–23 © Baileys Archive/africanpictures/The Image Works; pp. 24–25 API/Gamma-Rapho/Getty Images; p. 29 Mary Benson Estate/Sygma/Getty Images; pp. 30–31 Amana Images Inc/Getty Images; p. 33 Allan Tannenbaum/The LIFE Images Collection/Getty Images; p. 35 Wally McNamee/Corbis Historical/Getty Images; p. 36 Walter Dhladhla/AFP/Getty Images; pp. 38–39 Pierre-Philippe Marcou/AFP/Getty Images; p. 41 Louise Gubb/Corbis Historical/Getty Images; cover and interior pages stars pattern f-64 Photo Office/amanaimagesRF/Thinkstock.

Design: Brian Garvey; Layout: Ellina Litmanovich; Editor: Amelie von Zumbusch; Photo Researcher: Bruce Donnola